IMAGES
of America

SEQUOIA
NATIONAL PARK

E-2 Three Graces
Sequoia Nat'l. Park, Calif.

The Three Graces, standing beside the Crescent Meadow Road in the Giant Forest, echo the words of John Muir, an early writer about the grandest sequoia grove. In *Our National Parks,* Muir described the setting: "It extends, a magnificent growth of giants grouped in pure temple groves, ranged in colonnades along the sides of meadows, or scattered among the other trees, from the granite headlands overlooking the hot foothills and plains of the San Joaquin back to within a few miles of the old glacier fountains at an elevation of 5,000 to 8,400 feet above the sea." (Courtesy of Sequoia and Kings Canyon National Parks.)

ON THE COVER: Poised at the edge of the Giant Forest plateau, Moro Rock towers 3,000 feet above the Middle Fork of the Kaweah River. In this 1920s photograph, a group has assembled on the first landing of the staircase leading to the summit. In the background, on the far side of the canyon, Castle Rocks can be seen. (Courtesy of Sequoia and Kings Canyon National Parks.)

IMAGES
of America

SEQUOIA
NATIONAL PARK

Ward Eldredge

ARCADIA
PUBLISHING

Published by Arcadia Publishing
Charleston, South Carolina

Library of Congress Catalog Card Number: 2008922699

For all general information contact Arcadia Publishing at:
Telephone 843-853-2070
Fax 843-853-0044
E-mail sales@arcadiapublishing.com
For customer service and orders:
Toll-Free 1-888-313-2665

Visit us on the Internet at www.arcadiapublishing.com

This book is dedicated to the memory of Miriam Mantle Eldredge.

CONTENTS

ACKNOWLEDGMENTS

Most of the photographs in this book are from the archival collections of the Sequoia and Kings Canyon National Parks and represent the work of many photographers. First and foremost of these is Lindley Eddy, the photographic concessionaire at the Giant Forest for 30 years, whose work captured the early atmosphere of the forest and established a visual style for Sequoia National Park. Thanks are also due to the curators who saved and organized the approximately 20,000 images in the parks' collections. Most of this work was done by rangers, naturalists, botanists, and seasonal employees—the care and intelligence with which it was accomplished is a gift to the future. Susan Snyder provided access to the Kaweah Colony holdings of the Bancroft Library, University of California at Berkeley. Floyd Thomas, curator at the National Afro-American Museum and Cultural Center of Wilberforce, Ohio, shared the papers of Col. Charles Young. Mike Drake of the Tulare County Library provided assistance and useful images of George Stewart. And Ellen Byrne, of the Colby Library of the Sierra Club, has greatly enriched the chapter on Sequoia's backcountry. Two local historians, Sophie Britten and Louise Jackson, have each provided important assistance in understanding the contribution of the neighboring community of Three Rivers to the parks' history.

I also want to thank the interpretive team of the Sequoia and Kings Canyon National Parks with whom it has been my pleasure to work for the better part of the last decade. Thanks in particular to Colleen Bathe, chief of the Division of Interpretation, for her support. Tom Burge, the parks' archeologist, has been a steady source of good humor and historical insight. Malinee Crapsey, the parks' interpretive specialist and editor, has greatly enriched the present work with her skill and dedication. Bob Meadows has shared his encyclopedic knowledge of the park landscape. Emily Edgar, in the human resources office, provided important guidance in the early stages of this project. Athena Demetry, of the Division of Resource Management and Science, kindly offered to share her photographs of the ecological restoration of the Giant Forest, the culmination of nearly 75 years of study and planning. Lastly, I would like to thank William Tweed, who has never hesitated to share the knowledge he gained from a career spent studying the park, its environment, and its history. His generosity and thoughtfulness are a great source of encouragement.

Thanks also to John Poultney and Lori Gildersleeve at Arcadia Publishing for their enthusiasm for this project. Personal thanks are also due to my wife, Suzanne Bake, for her support and intelligence, and to my father, Howard Eldredge, for clarifying the dates of many images.

INTRODUCTION

On September 25, 1890, Pres. Benjamin Harrison signed legislation creating Sequoia National Park. The unusual nature of this action is easy to overlook, but it had only happened once before, 18 years previous, when Yellowstone Park was established from two million acres of the Great Geyser Basin in the Wyoming Territory.

By 1890, the frontier was gone, a railroad stretched from sea to sea, and the unbounded energy of decades of expansion was settling into new patterns. Unlike Yellowstone, Sequoia was no faraway outpost; this new park overlooked a heavily settled agricultural region. Yet the area was almost as unknown as Yellowstone, and its marvels were as astonishing.

Sequoia National Park was established to protect the rich forests of the western slope of the Sierra Nevada, the only place on earth to find *Sequoiadendron gigantean*—the giant sequoia. Called by John Muir "nature's forest masterpiece," the species was first described in the 1850s, and like early accounts of Yellowstone, descriptions were met with disbelief. In 1852, a hunter retained to provide fresh meat for the miners of Murphy's Camp tracked a wounded grizzly bear into a forest that astounded the imagination. The discovery soon caused a sensation. The following summer, the "Discovery Tree" was felled—not by saw, for none was large enough—but by successive holes drilled with a pump augur from the neighboring placer mines. A segment was sent for exhibition first in San Francisco and then New York City, with admission to see "The Mammoth Tree, the Vegetable Wonder of the World" to be bought for 50¢.

The Calaveras Grove became a popular destination, as did the groves to the south near Yosemite Valley, which had been set aside for protection in 1862 as a state park. A year later, John S. Hittel, a forty-niner-turned-San-Francisco-journalist, described in *The Resources of California* the otherworldly atmosphere of the Mariposa Grove:

> When in such forests, I have at times compared myself to a merman, who while at the bottom of the ocean, amid a large growth of queer seaweed, and surrounded by beautiful shells and the treasure of a thousand wrecks, should look from his abode of peace, and see the surface of the water, far above, raging in a terrific storm.

But the largest groves, with the largest trees, were further to the south. On a broad plateau above the canyons of the Middle and North Forks of the Kaweah River, and again on a ridge above the South Fork, grew the largest groves of all. The area was little known and seldom visited—the plateau is isolated on three sides by deep and rugged canyons and on the fourth by a mountain ridge. Immigrants settled in increasing numbers on the rich land along the broad alluvial fans of the rivers that drain the Sierra to the west—particularly on the broad delta of the Kaweah River, but the huge forests and upland meadows were known only to a few cattlemen and nomadic sheepherders.

One of the few visitors was John Muir, who, in 1875, followed the sequoia belt south from the Mariposa Grove. In his account of the trip, "On the Post-Glacial History of Sequoia Gigantea," published the following year in the *Proceedings of the American Association for the Advancement of Science*, Muir describes his journey south:

> Descending the precipitous divide between the Kings River and the Kaweah, we enter the colossal forests of the main continuous portion of the sequoia belt. As we advance southward, the trees become more and more impressibly exuberant, tossing their massive crowns against the sky from every ridge top, and waving onward in graceful compliance to the complicated topography of the basins of the Kaweah and the Tule.

On this trip, John Muir named the grandest of the groves "The Giant Forest"—the heart of what would become Sequoia National Park.

In the 1880s, agricultural interests began lobbying for protection of the Sierra forests. *Visalia Times* editor George Stewart lobbied throughout the 1880s for the importance of irrigation; he predicted that water "now going to waste will be brought to thirsty lands and made to reveal riches in comparison with which the gold and silver of the mines will appear of far less importance than now." To insure the steady supply of water, the forests needed protecting, and Stewart and his allies petitioned Congress. The year before passage of the bill creating the park, Stewart wrote in an editorial:

> There are many reasons why our forests should be preserved, and particularly those grand sequoias that have withstood the storms of centuries. It is sacrilege to destroy one of them. There are few who have not begun to realize the necessity of preserving [the trees] as they are the natural reservoirs that nature has placed above our great fertile plain, and so unanimous and earnest is the desire that the work of deforestation be at once stayed, that every friend of the San Joaquin Valley and every lover of the wild woodland may cherish the hope that congress will be induced to throw about our splendid forests at once the mantle of government protection.

For its first quarter century, Sequoia National Park was administered by no specialized agency. For its first dozen years, the park was patrolled in the summer months by U.S. Cavalry soldiers. With little direction or oversight, these soldiers forged a course of resource protection and park development based only upon their own initiative. As early as 1899, an acting superintendent, 2nd Lt. Henry Benjamin Clarke, reflected on the possibilities and promise of the national park:

> But what is a park—a national park? Is it a playground for the people, a resort for the tourist, a mecca for travelers, a summer house where the inhabitants of crowded cities can repair and fill their lungs with the pure air of mountain and forest—where poet, artist, clerk, and artisan, without discrimination, can stand on lofty peak and breathe the inspiration of scenes of grandeur?

The first step in the process was to provide access and welcome the visitor. As Clarke describes the giant sequoia in the conclusion of his report to the secretary of the interior:

> Here are the pyramids of America, the mammoths of the whole vegetable kingdom, and the descendents, the scientist tells us, of still mightier giants. It is well if their towering tops pierce the very clouds and the shade of their able trunks save the Sierra snows from April till June; but is this their greatest good? Should not these monsters of the mountains be known and seen and felt by an admiring people? It is time that a systematic development of the Sequoia National Park be inaugurated.

Today it is difficult to imagine an America without its national parks, a country in which these amazing places are not an ideal of the national character. Yet at the moment of Sequoia's creation in 1890, a park system idea was only forming, and the natural environment was more the source of individual wealth than collective benefit and enjoyment. The images that follow document not only the evolution of this idea, of national parks preserved for the many rather than the few, they also document a changing relationship with the natural world.

One

CREATING A
NATIONAL PARK

THE SIERRAS AS SEEN FROM HANFORD, TULARE COUNTY; 120 MILES IN THREE SECTIONS.
1. Mt. Lyell. 2. Mt. Ritter. 3. Mt. Goddard. 4. Mt. Silliman. 5. Mt Gardiner. 6. Mt. Brewer. 7. Mt. Tyndall. 8. Mt. Williamson. 9. Mt. Hazen. 10. Mt. Michaelis. 11. Milestone Mountain. 12. Mt. Langley. 13. Location of Mt. Whitney. 14. Mt. Abert. 15. Mt. Henry. 16. Mt. Le Conte. 17. Mt. Kaweah. 18. Empire Mountain. 19. Miner's Peak. 20. Mt. Garfield. 21. Bullion Peak.

In the 19th century, the peaks of the Sierra Nevada were both an obstacle and a boon. Separating the Great Central Valley from the rich mining districts to the east, the mountains also were the sole source of water for a valley increasingly given over to agriculture. The important role played by the rich forests on the western slope—slowing snow melt, holding moisture in the soil, and preventing erosion—was argued persistently and persuasively in area newspapers. This panorama was published in W. W. Elliott's *Grand and Sublime Scenery* in 1883. The concentration of peaks at the left edge of the bottom panel defines the Kaweah watershed, the backbone of today's Sequoia National Park. (Courtesy of the Bancroft Library, University of California, Berkeley.)

9

In these early days, the southern Sierra was the province of a few cattlemen and sheepherders who brought their animals in summer to feed on the high-country meadows. While sequoia groves to the north were already established tourist destinations, here where the groves and individual trees are the largest of all, they remained seldom visited. Then, in 1885, as this rough country was first surveyed and made available for purchase, a utopian collective from San Francisco applied for title. Their first and most important project was to construct a road to reach the vast timber reserves of the middle elevations. (Both, courtesy of the Bancroft Library, University of California, Berkeley.)

Using the profits from a collectively owned and operated logging enterprise, the Kaweah Co-operative Colony hoped to build a society based not on competition, but on cooperation. While the roadwork progressed, they founded a town site—Kaweah—near the confluence of the North and Middle Forks of the river. They also established a tent camp, called Advance, midway between Kaweah and the timber belt. In addition to the vegetable garden, Advance boasted a piano and a printing press.

After five years' labor, the road was finished, and a small mill was set up at the lower margin of the conifers. Then, just as logging commenced, the creation of Sequoia National Park brought the operation to a halt. For several years, the claims of the colony worked their way through the courts, eventually to be invalidated. (Courtesy of the Bancroft Library, University of California, Berkeley.)

Others were drawn to the region by hopes of mineral riches. Mineral King Valley, at the headwaters of the East Fork, was the scene of a short-lived speculative boom in the 1870s. In this photograph, taken in the 1930s, Boy Scouts stand on the remains of the bridge at the bottom of River Hill, the most difficult stretch of the old toll road.

Discovery of mineral-rich soils at the head of the valley triggered a frenzy of speculation in the 1870s and gave the valley its name. At the head of the valley, the old mining town of Beulah endured a decade of boom and bust.

The most elaborate and expensive venture at Mineral King Valley was the Empire Mine. A tramway to ferry the ore buckets down to the stamp mill was built by Andrew Hallidie, one of the originators of the San Francisco cable-car system. (Courtesy of the Mineral King Preservation Society.)

By the turn of the 20th century, little remained of the original town but the old Smith Hotel and Post Office. It was destroyed in 1906 by an avalanche triggered by the great San Francisco earthquake.

Some of the original prospectors, like Mary and Harry Trauger, settled along the Mineral King toll road. Their homestead, known as Last Chance, was a popular rest stop for travelers.

A little further up the road, in the conifers of the mid-montane forests, was a small piece of private property known as Atwell Mill. Hundreds of sequoias in the East Fork Grove were logged here between 1879 and 1920.

By the late 1870s, local newspaperman George Stewart was advocating for the protection of the Kaweah watershed and editorializing for the protection of the big trees. A group of prominent citizens of Tulare County, including Tipton Lindsey and J. D. Hyde of the General Land Office; Stewart; another staff member of the *Delta* named Frank W. Walker; D. K. Zumwalt, a local lawyer with ties to the Southern Pacific Railroad; and the prominent landowner John Tuohy, actively petitioned for the area's conservation. (Courtesy of the Annie R. Mitchell, Tulare County Library, Visalia, California)

The group argued that the threat posed by deforestation to the Kaweah watershed was grave enough to require the "permanent reservation"—removal from the market—of a substantial segment of the southern Sierra. By the 1880s, Visalia was the largest city in California south of Stockton, and its agricultural wealth was entirely dependent on rivers running with melting mountain snows. George Stewart is seen here in the 1920s with four of his allies in the campaign for conservation.

15

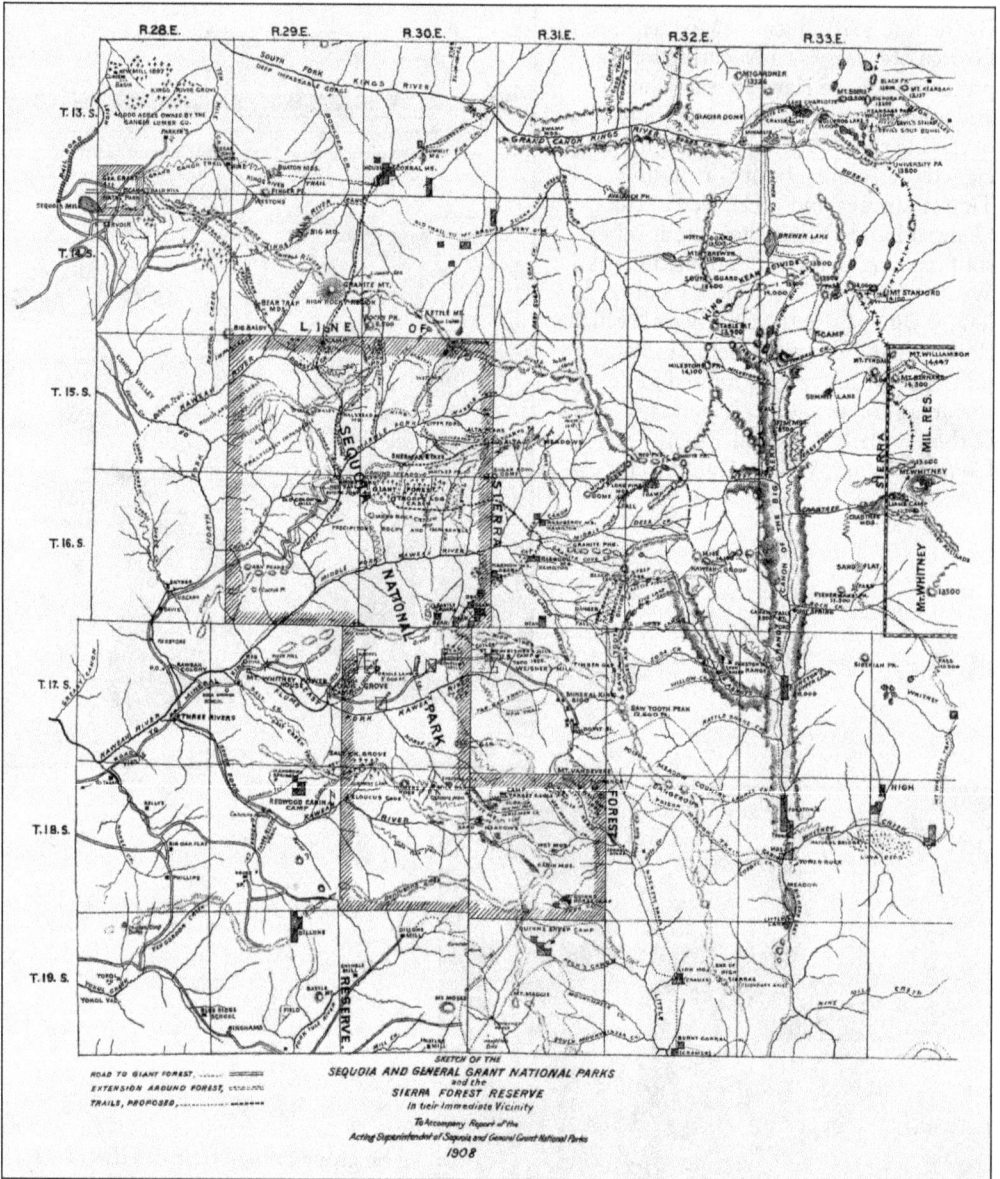

On September 25, 1890, President Harrison signed into law the creation of the country's second national park. One week later, the park was enlarged to include the largest-known sequoia grove—the Giant Forest.

The following summer of 1891 saw the arrival of two companies of U.S. Cavalry, sent by the Presidio of San Francisco to guard the new park. In this undated photograph, the troopers are seen heading down the canyon from the park through the neighboring town of Three Rivers. The cavalry would administer and protect the park for the next 12 years.

Often arriving before the higher elevations were free from snow, the cavalry usually camped in the foothills below the park for some weeks. Eventually, the troopers would relocate to Mineral King or Hockett Meadow. This photograph shows the temporary encampment at Red Hill on the Main Fork of the Kaweah River.

The heart of the new park was the Giant Forest, the largest un-logged grove of sequoias and home to five of the world's 10 largest trees. The first of the acting military superintendents, Capt. J. H. Dorst, wrote in his annual report to the secretary of the interior, "It is probably the most remarkable forest of its kind in the world. The more one sees of it the grander it seems. To despoil it would be a desecration."

The plateau of the Giant Forest is punctuated by a number of meadows, openings in which the full scale of the setting is more readily appreciated. A photograph from the *Annual Superintendent's Report 1900* shows a trooper at the edge of Crescent Meadow.

The cavalry, and the few visitors during that era, used the road built by the Kaweah Co-operative Colony to approach the Giant Forest. By 1900, when this photograph was taken, it had deteriorated so thoroughly as to be passable only to pack animals. The park's first ever appropriation of funds was dedicated that year to the improvement and completion of the road to the Giant Forest.

The following year saw the road extended past the heavy rock work above the old Colony Mill. Here the road crosses from the Yucca Creek drainage into the canyon of the Marble Fork of the Kaweah.

In 1903, the park was patrolled by buffalo soldiers under the command of Col. (then a captain) Charles Young of the 9th U.S. Cavalry. The third African American graduate of West Point, Young's tenure in the park was remarkable for its energetic accomplishments. (Courtesy of the National Afro-American Museum and Cultural Center, Wilberforce, Ohio.)

The most significant achievement of the summer was the completion of the road to the Giant Forest. This was celebrated with an open-air banquet for the road crew and invited guests from Visalia, including newspaperman George Stewart. Charles Young predicted that the new road would "insure a thousand tourists where in previous years there have been but a hundred." (Courtesy of the National Afro-American Museum and Cultural Center, Wilberforce, Ohio.)

In this group portrait taken at the 1903 banquet, Charles Young is front and center. Behind him is George "Grandpa" Welch, the road foreman; to Welch's immediate right, in the three-piece suit, is a member of the crew, Walter Fry, who would go on to become one of the park's first civilian rangers and its first non-military superintendent. Between the two is George Stewart.

The invited guests proposed naming a sequoia tree for Colonel Young, but Young demurred, instead authorizing the naming of one for "that great and good American" Booker T. Washington. This tree was relocated and rededicated in the centennial year of Young's superintendency, 2003. (Courtesy of Forest History Society, Durham, North Carolina.)

With the completion of the road in 1903, Young understood the increased threat to the trees—compacted soil from foot, hoof, and wheel, and bark peeled away by eager souvenir hunters. He built a fence around the largest and most famous sequoia of all, the General Sherman Tree. Unfortunately, the fence only lasted a few years and was not replaced until the 1920s. Young also obtained options for the numerous pieces of private property within the grove, but funds were not made available for their purchase.

Some of Young's troopers were dispatched to the Sierra Crest, where they assisted with the construction of the first trail to the summit of Mount Whitney, the highest point in the contiguous United States. This photograph from Young's personal papers shows Army Pass just south of Whitney. The name of the pass, as well as that of nearby Soldier Lake, is most likely a remembrance of the cavalry's work in the vicinity. (Courtesy of the National Afro-American Museum and Cultural Center.)

In 1913, the last year of military administration, troopers under the command of Lt. Hugh Johnson posed in front of the General Sherman Tree. For its first 23 summers, the foundations of the national park were established by soldiers with little direct oversight and little funding. Their success is a tribute to the ingenuity and creativity of the individual commanders.

The cavalry protected the forest from private economic interests while providing access to the public.

Hired in 1900, Ernest Britten was the first civilian ranger in Sequoia National Park. Britten, and those that followed, provided local knowledge and an important degree of continuity. He is pictured here along with his wife, Mary Sivertsen Britten.

By 1906, the civilian ranger force had grown to four permanent, year-round rangers. From left to right, they are L. L. Davis, Walter Fry, Ernest Britten's nephew Harry, and Charles Blossom.

Found at the northern edge of the Giant Forest, the General Sherman Tree is the largest tree on earth—270 feet tall and 30 feet in diameter. It was named in 1879 by cattleman James Wolverton, a veteran of the Civil War with Sherman's 9th Indiana Cavalry. A branch fell from the tree in 2005 with a diameter larger than that of any tree east of the Mississippi

The partnership of John Broder and Ralph Hopping operated a stage line from the valley railroad station at Lemon Cove to the Giant Forest. Later the line was operated by the River Inn Hotel Company and later yet by J. A. Mehrton. Here the coach passes between the Four Guardsmen, heralds of the arrival to the Giant Forest.

'Around the campfire'. Camp Sierra, Giant Forest.

Beginning around 1905, tent cabins were available to rent. Camp Sierra, seen here in the 1910s, changed hands a number of times as it continued to grow along the northern margin of Round Meadow. It would eventually come to be known as the Giant Forest Lodge.

Other visitors were left largely to their own devices and were free to set up camp at any number of camping areas. Rustic camping facilities were established throughout the Giant Forest and at the edges of meadows, and were nestled amongst the ferns, willows, and dogwoods beside Hazelwood Creek.

At first, visitors to the Giant Forest were usually local people seeking an escape from the summer heat of the Central Valley. Of the 5,000 visitors to the park in 1915, nearly 4,300 came from California. The difficult journey led many visitors to establish semipermanent camps where they

would stay the entire summer. The Hammond family, from the nearby town of Tulare, came every year. This photograph of their camp was taken around 1917.

Here in the Giant Forest, residents of neighboring communities established a relationship with the natural environment that would be passed down from generation to generation. Such local involvement is one of the distinguishing characteristics of Sequoia National Park.

In 1911, more than 3,000 people visited the park. One visitor, Dorothy (Zumwalt) Thompson, kept a photo album of her trip to the park that year. Travelling with her father and several cousins, Zumwalt was celebrating her graduation from a high school in Tulare. On July 7, the party arrived by train at Lemon Cove and transferred to saddle and carriage.

Like many to follow, the Zumwalt group paused for a photograph at the first giant sequoias they came upon.

From a camp at Little Willow Meadow, the group visited the principal sights. They scrambled up onto the massive granite dome of Moro Rock to witness the grand views of Middle Fork Canyon and the high country to the east.

The Zumwalt group also climbed over Panther Gap toward the summit of Alta Peak. The caption for this photograph reads "my first snow."

On the summit of Alta Peak, at 11,700 feet, the group experienced the space and silence of the high places.

In 1916, Congress created the National Park Service (NPS). Within the first year, superintendent Walter Fry would establish two of the park's iconic experiences. One was a series of wooden steps leading to the summit of Moro Rock. While safer than the scramble they replaced, the steps must still have afforded a considerable thrill—creaky, swaying, and with a handrail on only one side.

Walter Fry stands on the last flight of the new steps near the summit. A trip to the top of Moro Rock was, and remains, one of the quintessential experiences of Sequoia National Park. The first guidebook assured visitors: "The climb up the 162 steps is thrilling but at no point dangerous." Today's steps, built in 1931, are made of concrete.

The Auto Log. Giant Forest.

The Auto Log was the second of Walter Fry's constructions. For many decades, it provided a unique and popular photo opportunity. When a 2,000-year-old giant sequoia was blown over by a windstorm in February 1917, Fry had a trestle built so that vehicles might be driven atop the log. In a report to the secretary of the interior, Fry described how the fallen log was adapted for a novel use: "It now lies almost parallel to the road, and automobiles can be taken upon its prostrate form with little difficulty. It has afforded much amusement for motorists during the summer. Automobiles can be operated over the tree for a distance of over 200 feet, and 20 small cars can be driven upon the tree at the same time."

At the turn of the 20th century, there were 8,000 automobiles registered in the United States; by 1920, about when this photograph of the General Sherman Tree was taken, that number had swelled to nearly nine and a half million. The arrival of the automobile to the Giant Forest would bring waves of new visitors—and visitors from farther away. It would also pose new and unforeseen challenges.

In 1920, Sequoia National Park was poised between two eras. On one side stood the quietude of the past, and on the other, the rush of the future.

Two

A DECADE OF GROWTH

By 1920, when the first detailed trail map was published, the visitor to the Giant Forest would find a system of roads, trails, and attractions. The road from Visalia led to the concentration of buildings and camps encircling Round Meadow. From here, a series of secondary roads radiated outwards to Sunset Rock, north to end at the camp on the banks of the Marble Fork, and south and west to Moro Rock and Crescent Meadow.

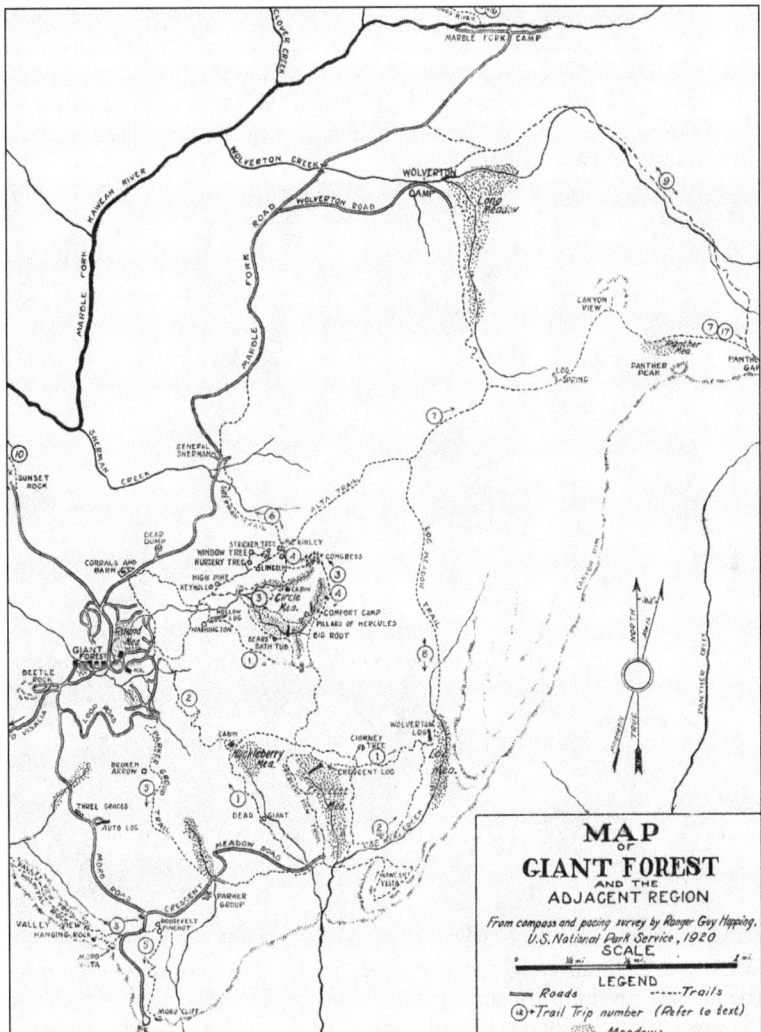

MAP
OF
GIANT FOREST
AND THE
ADJACENT REGION

From compass and pacing survey by Ranger Guy Hopping,
U.S. National Park Service, 1920

SCALE

LEGEND

Roads   Trails
(14) Trail Trip number (Refer to text)
Meadows

On July 27, 1920, a picnic was held to celebrate the arrival of a new superintendent, Col. John R. White. Known as "the Colonel," White was an Englishman by birth. A veteran of the Spanish-American War and the subsequent occupation of the Philippines, he would bring great energy to park management.

White was a common sight on horseback in the Giant Forest. He was responsible for modernizing the facilities and infrastructure of the park, but he came to see the dangers of overdevelopment. He was personally involved in all aspects of the park for nearly 25 years.

A visitor in the 1920s would find the Giant Forest a busy place. Clustered along the northern edge of Round Meadow, the lodge with its rustic dining hall was the clear focus of activity.

Across the meadow, at the original village, were a post office, a store, and Lindley Eddy's photographic studio.

Commercial pack-train outfits were available for trips into the high country. In the background is the original Giant Forest Post Office near Round Meadow.

Camping throughout the grove was eventually organized into six campgrounds: Highlands, Firwood, Paradise, Sunset Rock, Sugar Pine, and Hazelwood.

By the 1920s, visitors were arriving almost exclusively by personal car. Here a group drives up to the dining hall of the Giant Forest Lodge.

On July 4, 1922, an impromptu softball game took place in Round Meadow. The crowd was made up of campers and lodgers from the facilities that literally ringed the meadow.

The park's earliest programs were pageants, most famously *Ersa of the Red Trees*. The play is set in a forest protected by an ailing king but threatened by foreign forces seeking to log the great trees. Ersa, the king's daughter, must endure a curse, which each month turns her into a beautiful—and hunted—golden bird. Brought to Sequoia in 1922, the play was a considerable success. Beginning in 1928, it was performed annually, and at night, Col. John R. White described how the atmosphere was amplified by "the delightful lighting effects."

In the program of the 1931 production, Col. John R. White reflected on the educational significance of such productions: "The preservation of at least a semblance of wildness, of natural conditions, of flowers, shrubs and trees unspoiled by the thousands who pass by where but one or two came in the horse and buggy days—that preservation of flora and fauna is perhaps the principle problem of a park superintendent. 'Ersa of the Red Trees,' presented by Floyd Byrnes' Players has symbolized the age and majesty of the giant sequoias in such a manner as to make a popular appeal to those who might scarcely see warning signs or read the park regulations."

Traveling the Old Colony Mill Road by automobile—a narrow wagon road—was a genuine adventure. The morning was reserved for uphill traffic, the afternoon for downhill. This 1924 photograph, taken near the old Kaweah town site, shows the traffic control sign and the "Kaweah Road Control Kar" waiting to escort visitors the 20 dusty miles to the Giant Forest.

As the old wagon road started to climb, it passed through a gate at the park boundary.

In this 1920s photograph, automobiles have assembled in the old Giant Forest Museum parking lot to wait for an escort for the downhill journey.

In the summer of 1921, construction began on a new road to the Giant Forest. The new route was to follow the Middle Fork of the Kaweah River to Hospital Rock and then climb the slopes below Moro Rock via a series of switchbacks. While the road was being designed for automobiles, not horses and buggies, at least some of the work was being accomplished with traditional hand tools.

A steam shovel was also employed for the heavy rock work encountered on the long climb to the Giant Forest. In the background is Castle Rocks on the far side of the Middle Fork Canyon.

James B. Small, the road construction foreman, is given credit for "One Shot Rock"—a massive granite boulder cleaved in two by a single shot of dynamite.

In the summer of 1926, after nearly 10 years of planning and five years of construction, the Generals Highway was opened between the foothills and the Giant Forest. The dedication took place at the new entrance to the park in the Middle Fork Canyon.

Following the ceremony, a picnic like the one served in 1903 was held in the Giant Forest. In this photograph, the director of the National Park Service, Stephen Mather, and his daughter, Bertha Mather McPherson, are sitting across the table from George Welch, the construction foreman for the Old Colony Mill Road, as Col. John R. White (standing, left) and Visalia publisher and businessman Ben Maddox look on.

Stephen Mather, the first director of the National Park Service, was an inveterate promoter. The rapid growth and great success of the fledgling agency was in large part due to his vision.

Generals Highway from Moro Rock - Sequoia Nat'l Park, Calif.

The new road followed the Middle Fork of the Kaweah River before climbing nearly 4,000 vertical feet through a series of switchbacks to the Giant Forest. In this postcard, the ribbon of highway is seen from Moro Rock.

Designed for automobile traffic, the new road was built on a gentler grade and with a smoother surface than the old—and it had two lanes. Unpaved, the new road still offered a dusty trip. Mono Rock can be seen in the distance.

The summer the new road opened, park visitation rose by 150 percent. Congestion was the result in many park areas, including the Moro Rock parking lot.

The automobile not only brought scores of new visitors, but it also substantially changed the impact of these visits on the forest.

P-16 Houskeeping under the Big Trees - Sequoia Nat'l. Park. Calif.

Park visitation would increase from 19,000 in 1919 to 111,000 in 1929. In the summer of 1929, nine thousand visitors stayed overnight in park accommodations. Many stayed in "housekeeping cabins," to which visitors were expected to bring their own kitchenware and linens.

Another 20,000 stayed in the Giant Forest's campgrounds. This photograph from the mid-1930s was taken in the Hazelwood Campground.

opted Baby - Sequoia Nat'l. Park, Calif.

In the first flush of development, the harmful repercussions of feeding the wildlife were not yet fully understood. While such behavior would be discouraged today, these two images can be seen as examples of the bond with the natural world that was formed by visitors to the Giant Forest.

E-14 "Pals" - Sequoia Nat'l. Park, Calif.

To absorb the rise in visitation, the park reorganized the commercial center of the Giant Forest. A new site was prepared, and park buildings that had been scattered around the margins of Round Meadow were relocated on the opposite side of the new highway near the Moro Rock Road junction.

The Giant Forest Village was laid out along a large plaza and included a market, a lunchroom, a photo studio, and a gas station.

The centerpiece of the new plaza of the Giant Forest Village, designed by the architect Gilbert Stanley Underwood and completed in 1929, was the Giant Forest Market. In 2001, following the ecological restoration of the Giant Forest, the market was rededicated as a visitors' center, interpreting the history of the grove and the ecology of the giant sequoia.

The village was also the site of Lindley Eddy's photography studio. For 25 years, Eddy was the photographer of the Giant Forest, creating hundreds of images for postcards and other mementos, and documenting all manner of park events. The richness and high esthetic of the park's early photographic history is due in large measure to his efforts and skill.

Remaining at Round Meadow was Walter Fry's museum, the hub of the park's education efforts.

At the museum, visitors could examine a three-dimensional relief map of the park's topography, study botanical specimens, and join a guided walk.

A self-taught naturalist, Walter Fry knew more about the sequoias and the Giant Forest than anyone else alive. In 1920, "the grand old man of the sequoias" was appointed district magistrate. In his spare time, he began leading guided walks, initiated the creation of the park's museum collection, and published articles on the region's human and natural history. A principle figure of the park's early history, Fry is remembered as the founder of both the ranger-naturalist and the museum programs.

In this 1927 photograph, Walter Fry lectures to a group that is dwarfed by the scale of the General

Sherman Tree.

The nature-guide program continued to grow, and in 1929, Frank Been was hired as Sequoia National Park's first full-time ranger-naturalist. In this 1930 photograph, Been has led a group to the first landing on the steps of Mono Rock.

Been led guided walks throughout the Giant Forest and points further afield. Here, at Heather Lake, one of the most accessible of the southern Sierra's innumerable alpine lakes, a group is introduced to the glaciated granite of Tokopah Canyon and the Tablelands.

By the end of the decade, the usefulness of the nature guides was well established. In July of that year alone, the nature guides conducted 40 field trips attended by 1,059 visitors and gave 88 lectures to a cumulative audience of over 10,000.

As district magistrate, Walter Fry was sometimes called upon in his capacity of justice of the peace. Here Judge Fry performs a marriage in Crescent Meadow.

In 1930, director Raoul Walsh filmed the last scenes of his motion picture *The Big Trail* in the Giant Forest. A saga of western migration, the film starred Marguerite Churchill and, in his first leading role, a young John Wayne. Here the lead actors pause for a portrait with Col. John R. White (center).

Raoul Walsh filmed the entire movie on location. The film cost $2 million and took four months to complete. The production traveled 2,000 miles, filming in Montana, Wyoming, and Utah before reaching California.

After surviving the perils of the trek westward, *The Big Trail* ends with the settlers homesteading beside one of the Giant Forest's meadows.

Director Ralph Walsh returned to the Giant Forest in 1932 to film a second movie, constructing an elaborate set near the lodge dining hall. *Wild Girl,* or *Salomy Jane,* starred Joan Bennett, and for two weeks, the Giant Forest Lodge was booked solid with 115 employees of the Fox Film Corporation.

Between 1915 and 1920, the park managed to purchase all of the small pieces of private property within the Giant Forest. When public moneys fell short, the National Geographic Society (NGS) and members of the Sierra Club made timely donations that enabled the purchase. On July 10, 1927, a plaque commemorating their support was dedicated at Round Meadow. Present are Judge Walter Fry, unidentified, NPS director Stephen Mather, NGS representative Ralph Phelps (kneeling), Col. John R. White, Congressman H. E. Barbour, state senator W. F. Chandler, Sierra Club members William Colby and Aurelia Harwood, and one of the park's naturalists portraying the "spirit of sequoia."

The day of July 4, 1930, saw the most visitors to ever visit the park up to that point—1,176 cars and 4,256 visitors. Col. John R. White (standing, second from right) and assistant chief ranger Ford Spigelmyre (standing, far right) enlisted a group of children—a "white-wing brigade"—to help with the clean-up. In half a day, the boys collected over a ton of cans and trash.

Pioneer Hale Tharp settled along the Main Fork of the Kaweah River in the late 1850s, and in the summer, he pastured his cattle in the meadows of the Giant Forest. Here, beside Log Meadow, Tharp fashioned a fallen sequoia log into a rustic cabin. In this 1921 photograph, Ira Clayton, who decades earlier had worked for Tharp and lived in the cabin, is seated beside a park service landscape architect. Over the course of the next year, Clayton would assist in the restoration of Tharp's Log.

At the dedication of Tharp's Log, a photograph of Hale Tharp was present, as were members of the Three Rivers Women's Association, whose donations made the restoration work possible.

On June 26, 1938, a giant sequoia near the Giant Forest Museum was dedicated as a living memorial to a pioneer of women's suffrage, Susan B. Anthony.

Col. John R. White, in a radio address, said of Susan B. Anthony: "Her accomplishments were so far reaching, it seems most fitting to have her memory perpetuated by an evergrowing and everlasting monument—such as this Sequoia Gigantea. . . . The sequoia tree named in Miss Anthony's honor is probably 3,000 years old now. Its life span has already embraced most of the history of mankind—and it will probably still be living to see undreamed of changes and advancements in a yet unborn civilization."

After the dedication, a reception was held at the superintendent's house in the Giant Forest. Guests included secretary of the interior Harold Ickes; NPS director Arno Cammerer; senator William Gibbs McAdoo; and California governor Frank Merriam.

Some individual sequoia trees, like the General Sherman Tree, were named before the park was created. Most, however, like the Senate Group, were named in the 1920s, the principal years of park development. The House and Senate Groups—together called the Congress Group—were named by chief ranger Guy Hopping.

In 1938, Sequoia National Park capitalized on a fallen sequoia blocking the Crescent Meadow Road to create the Tunnel Log. The park has never had a standing, "drive-through" tree; the most famous of these, the Wawona Tree in Yosemite's Mariposa Grove, fell over in a windstorm in 1969.

Impervious to fire and pests, sequoias are without natural threats, and many of the older trees are more than 3,000 years old. If a sequoia dies, it is because it has fallen over. This tree blocked a rail in the Hazelwood Campground.

With the completion of the new
highway, the park was for the first
time accessible year-round.

In 1934, to promote winter visitation, the park, the Sequoia National Park Company, and the Visalia Chamber of Commerce held an annual Winter Sports Carnival. The 1936 event, shown here, featured a ski race and the crowning of the queen of the carnival.

The Winter Sports Carnival proved hugely successful, and parking lots overflowed.

The carnival was held at Lodgepole, a new campground created to the north of the Giant Forest at the site of the old Marble Fork camp, which was built to ease congestion among the big trees. At this new location outside the sequoia grove, the park maintained a skating rink in the winter and a swimming hole in the summer.

With the establishment of Lodgepole Camp outside of the sequoia grove, the park began to address the negative impact of so much development upon the Giant Forest.

If the 1920s had been a decade of headlong growth in Sequoia National Park, the 1930s were an era of emergent conservation, characterized by more ecologically oriented management. While all of his battles were not victorious, Col. John R. White articulated a clear vision for America's national parks: "We should boldly ask ourselves whether we want the national parks to duplicate the features and entertainments of other resorts, or whether we want them to stand for something distinct, and we hope better in our national life."

Three

THE HIGH AND SILENT PLACES

From the Owens Valley on the east side of the Sierra, Mount Whitney forms part of one of the grandest escarpments in North America. The peak itself is the highest point in the contiguous United States, 14,494 feet above sea level. It is one of four peaks within a five-mile radius reaching over 14,000 feet, a fact that proved frustrating to the early surveyors of the Sierra Crest. In 1864, the California State Geological Survey, under the authority of state geologist Josiah Whitney, was exploring the region when two members, Clarence King and Richard Cotter, broke away in hopes of reaching the highest summit in the range. After two days of hard climbing, King related his sentiments at gaining the summit in his book, *Mountaineering in the Sierra Nevada*: "To our surprise, upon sweeping the horizon with my level, there appeared two peaks equal in height with us, and two rising even higher. . . . Mount Whitney, as we afterwards called it in honor of our chief, is probably the highest land within the United States. Its summit looked glorious, but inaccessible."

By the first years of the 20th century, adventurers were ranging throughout the High Sierra, and an organization, based in San Francisco, had been created to promote the enjoyment and exploration of the mountains: the Sierra Club. Several of their annual outings—enormous trips often requiring hundreds of pack animals—went into the southern Sierra. In 1904, they visited the Kern Canyon, the grand glacial valley between the Great Western Divide and the Sierra Crest, to camp in the wilds and ascend as many peaks as time allowed. In this 1904 photograph, members of the group are shown ascending Mount Williamson, located some miles north of Mount Whitney and only slightly less lofty a peak. (*Sierra Club Bulletin, Vol. 5.*)

Mount Williamson lies just east of the main Sierra Crest and is the peak visible in the distance of the above photograph. An account from the *Sierra Club Bulletin* described the climb: "Entering at the foot of one of these chimneys, our way led upward for 2,500 feet, at times over snow-patches, again climbing with hands and feet on the rocks bordering the slope, at times—and here most guardedly—zigzagging across and back over the insecure, shifting floor of the chimney, where a step loosed masses of broken talus, and great rocks, started at a touch, went leaping and bounding to a resting-place at the base of the mountain." The writer found the view from the summit (pictured below) grander than that from Whitney, as it "includes a view of majestic Whitney itself." (*Sierra Club Bulletin, Vol. 5.*)

By 1909, the highest point in the nation was seeing a lot of activity. Aside from the mountaineers, the Smithsonian Institution was arranging the construction of an atmospheric observatory and shelter on the summit. The instrument to the left was used to produce spectrographs of the atmosphere of Mars. (*Sierra Club Bulletin, Vol. 7.*)

In 1912, the Sierra Club's annual outing again traveled to the Kern Canyon. They departed, as had Capt. Charles Young nine years earlier, over Army Pass. "There was much ado about the trail, which was dug out of the snow with tin cups, one shovel and botany pick, and was trampled down by willing feet." These early trips were instrumental in forming a new type of relationship between a largely urban population and the Sierra wilderness. The participants took away nothing but photographs and memories "of the high and silent places, of starry nights and drowsy rooms beside the running waters, of forests and flower gardens and great enduring rock, new strength for old ideals, new ideals to try our strength." (*Sierra Club Bulletin, Vol. 9.*)

In 1915, the soon-to-be director of the National Park Service, Stephen Mather, organized and led a group of prominent men through the region in hopes of inspiring support for the national park idea. Members included a number of popular authors and journalists, a vice president of the Southern Pacific Railroad, a ranking member of the House Appropriations Committee, and the president of the National Geographic Society. The party traveled from Visalia to the Giant Forest and on to Mineral King Valley, where they made the long climb to Franklin Pass.

Descending from Franklin Pass via Rattlesnake Creek into the Kern Canyon, the Mather party traveled over the summit of Mount Whitney (pictured above and below) and down to Owens Valley. By the end of the following summer, the National Park Service would exist with Stephen Mather as its director.

A local woman played an instrumental role in the 1920s campaign to enlarge Sequoia National Park beyond the Giant Forest area to include the high country to the east. Susan Thew, with a hired photographer in tow, crisscrossed the High Sierra, creating an extraordinary photographic record of the region. These photographs she then organized and published, distributing copies of the resulting gazetteer to every member of Congress. Ansel Adams and the Sierra Club would utilize a similar strategy 10 years later in the campaign to protect Kings Canyon.

Two photographs from Susan Thew's gazetteer allowed legislators to see the nature of the landscapes proposed for protection. Pictured above is the view east across the headwaters of the Middle Fork of the Kaweah River toward the Great Western Divide and the Kaweah Group. Pictured below is the region east of Mineral King and the string of lakes below Sawtooth Peak: Columbine, Cyclamen, and Spring.

On July 3, 1926, Pres. Calvin Coolidge signed the legislation that more than doubled the size of Sequoia National Park. Here the sponsor of the bill, Congressman Henry Barbour, is given the key to the park by Col. John R. White (right).

East of the Great Western Divide is the Chagoopa Plateau and Moraine Lake. In this 1917 photograph by Walter Huber, the view west across the lake reflects the Kaweah Group. (*Sierra Club Bulletin, Vol. 10.*)

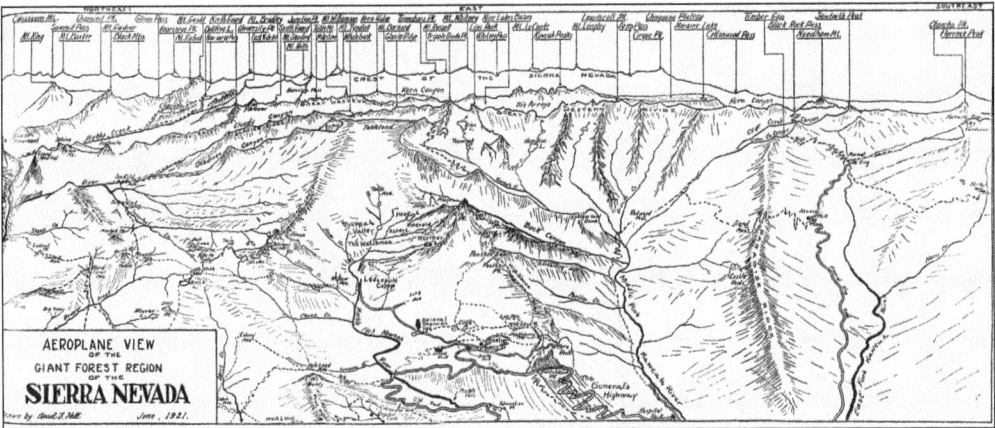

With the 1926 enlargement, the park now extended to the Sierra Crest and encompassed vast expanses of alpine wilderness.

Looking east from the steps to Moro Rock, all the eye could see was now parkland, protected in perpetuity.

This 1928 photograph by Ansel Adams shows the western slopes of Black Kaweah, the highest point west of the Kern River in the enlarged park. (*Sierra Club Bulletin, Vol. 13.*)

The Hamilton Lake basin is considered one of the most scenic spots in the Sierra Nevada. The naturally fishless lakes were stocked with fish by a homesteader, James Hamilton, who ran cattle in the Kaweah Canyon below at Redwood Meadow.

The enlargement of the park fundamentally changed the nature and scope of park operations. Here a ranger posts a boundary sign at Elizabeth Pass, at the headwaters of Lone Pine Creek, on the divide between the Kaweah and Kings Rivers watersheds. On a typical horse patrol, a ranger would be out for days at a time, often travelling 20 miles per day.

Ranger stations were established throughout the park's backcountry. The earliest of these, Quinn Horse Camp Station, was built in 1907. In this 1936 photograph, a group of rangers has assembled beside the station. They are, from left to right, unidentified, Ford Spigelmyre, Gaynell Brooks, Hugh Parkes, and George Brooks (partially hidden).

94

For many, being a ranger became a way of life. Ranger George Brooks and his wife, Gaynell, are seen here at the Clough Cave Station on the South Fork of the Kaweah River in the spring of 1929. Brooks worked in the backcountry of Sequoia for 30 years. At his retirement in 1950, Brooks recalled the work was "not peaches" but was varied and active, including patrolling, fighting fires, and, in the years before radio, repairing telephone lines.

In the summer of 1927, a new backcountry station was constructed at the southern end of the canyon near where the Kern River crosses the park boundary. Col. John R. White is seen inspecting the completed work.

Upon enlargement, the park's first priority was to provide access to the new territory. Col. John R. White became increasingly adamant in his opposition to both the expense and the damage that would be incurred by further road construction. Instead, White oversaw the creation of a network of mountain trails, opening the backcountry to hikers and stock, while preserving

its wild character. White wrote: "There is unanimity of opinion that the Kern Canyon and High Sierra area should be developed only as a trail park and that the honk of the motor horn should never echo in the, at present, almost virgin Yosemites of the enlarged park."

A large-scale coordinated effort to provide trail access to the Kern Canyon began almost immediately. Along the Sierra Crest, in a shared effort with the U.S. Forest Service, crews began building a permanent trail from Owens Valley to the summit of Mount Whitney and down into the Kern Canyon from the crest. In this July 1930 photograph, the crew rests beneath the Keeler Pinnacles on the precipitous eastern face of Mount Whitney.

The Whitney trail crew's construction camp, far above the timberline at an elevation approaching 14,000 above sea level, was in so remote a location that drinking water needed to be packed in.

The famed Sierran alpinist Norman Clyde (left front), who was the first to climb more than 100 peaks in the Sierra Nevada, worked on the Whitney trail crew in the summer of 1930.

Here a small crew is working high on the slopes of Mount Whitney at Trail Crest. In the background is the escarpment of Mount Hitchcock and, 3,000 feet below, Hitchcock Lakes.

In September 1930, a group assembled in Owens Valley to ascend the Mount Whitney Trail and celebrate its dedication. It was an opportunity to commemorate both the opening of the Sierran backcountry and its reservation as a road-less wilderness area. The group of 150 included representatives of the U. S. Forest Service, the Automobile Club of Southern California, various local chambers of commerce, and the film cameras of Pathé News. The group climbed the new switchbacks—heavily built to withstand winter snows—up nearly a vertical mile to Trail Crest.

From Trail Crest, the group followed the new director of the National Park Service, Horace Albright, along the spur trail to the summit—the highest point on the continental United States.

A press release from August 15, 1930, described the trail work and its place in the broader objectives of the park: "The construction of this trail to the summit of Mount Whitney has been going forward for several years under many difficulties of weather and altitude, and is part of a large trail construction program in Sequoia National Park which will render accessible by high class trails the best scenic and recreational spots in the Kern watershed. This area is reserved for a trail park in which no roads will be built."

The idea of a trail along the backbone of the Sierra to connect Yosemite Valley and Mount Whitney originated in the earliest days of the Sierra Club. In 1914, with the death of John Muir, the trail was conceived of as a memorial to that great friend of the mountains, and the following year, state funding was obtained. Forester Pass was blasted through in the summer of 1932, connecting Center Basin in the Kings River watershed with the headwaters of the Kern. Here, in a photograph by Walter Huber, travelers have dismounted, and the pack animals have been unhitched before descending the new trail.

From the west, the park began planning the High Sierra Trail. Beginning at Crescent Meadow, the route heads east along the upper slopes of the Middle Fork Canyon. Crossing first Buck Creek and then Lone Pine Creek, the trail climbs into the Hamilton Lake basin, named "Valhalla" by Col. John R. White. From there, it climbs to cross Kaweah Gap before the long descent down the Big Arroyo to the Kern River. In this 1929 photograph, (from left to right) NPS director Horace Albright, trail engineer John Diehl, and White consider the route.

The work required a jackhammer and compressor, as well as extensive blasting, and was engineered to establish an entirely new standard for recreational trails.

Mt. Stewart
Elev. 12202

On April 30, 1929, a peak on the Great Western Divide was named for George W. Stewart. Acknowledged as the father of Sequoia National Park, Stewart had used his position in the late 1880s as publisher of the *Visalia Delta* newspaper to lobby for the creation of the park. Stewart moved to Sacramento in 1927 but remained actively involved in park matters.

On the steps of the county courthouse in Visalia, NPS director Horace Albright points out the location of the peak to its namesake, George Stewart (far left).

On the slopes of Mount Stewart above Hamilton Lake can be seen Hamilton Gorge—the dark chasm just to the right of center in this image. This 125-foot-wide avalanche chute posed the High Sierra Trail's greatest engineering obstacle.

Col. John R. White was actively involved in all aspects of the planning for the High Sierra Trail. Here he contemplates the route around Hamilton Gorge.

106

One of trail engineer John Diehl's photographs—looking back across the lake from within the gorge—shows the extent of the challenge.

By the end of the construction season of 1932, a bridge would be built to span the 125 feet of Hamilton Gorge. All in all, more than 41,000 pounds of steel, cement, lumber, and tools were packed into the bridge site. Over 205 pack-animal loads were necessary before the rivet crew and foreman could begin work. A month later, on October 10, the crew laid asphalt on the steel floor of the bridge, and the High Sierra Trail was, for all intents and purposes, complete. Unfortunately, the bridge only lasted a few years; it was destroyed by an avalanche during the winter of 1937–1938.

In August 1932, Col. John R. White and his family took a pack trip to inspect the progress. As the bridge was not yet completed, White and his party were ferried across Hamilton Gorge by "high-line"—a cable strung across the chasm to transport equipment and materials. This photograph shows trail foreman John T. McDonald accompanying the superintendent's wife, Faye.

Beyond the gorge and Kern Canyon, Col. John R. White and his party ascended Mount Whitney from the west, traveling up the new trail and down the old. The comparison between the two was stark. The new trail, along Wallace Creek, was on an eight-percent grade and of a comfortable width.

The old trail, along Tyndall Creek, was on a 30- to 40-percent grade and was built, as Col. John R. White described, "just straight down the mountain."

At Kaweah Gap, the White party installed a plaque dedicated to the memory of George Stewart. One of the most spectacular stretches of trail in the park climbs and crosses the flank of Mount Stewart before reaching Kaweah Gap, with views back down Middle Fork Canyon and on to the Sierra Crest. Stewart and his wife, Martha, both passed away in the summer of 1932, and their ashes were interred here on the slopes of the mountain that bears their name.

In 1933, George Mauger, the general manager of the Giant Forest Lodge, traveled out the High Sierra Trail and chose the location for a high sierra camp at Bearpaw Meadow. With commanding views across Lone Pine Canyon, the camp celebrated its 75th anniversary in 2008, offering wilderness lodging in a breathtaking setting.

Seen here near its beginning at Crescent Meadow, the High Sierra Trail is a tangible aspect of Col. John R. White's enduring legacy of preservation. He wrote: "It is, of course, unnecessary to point out to any real lover of the out of doors that the benefits to be derived from trail travel are much greater than those from automobile travel; that is to say, that the trail travelers not only stay longer in the park, but they carry away from the park much better impressions and benefit physically and spiritually more by their visit to the park. These are, of course, intangibles, but due weight should be given them."

Four

THE FIRST
HALF-CENTURY

The new headquarters complex at Ash Mountain is seen from Yucca Point in 1927. Just left of center is the main administration building and the new entrance kiosk.

Prior to the 1920s, a maintenance road built by a local utility company to construct and service a hydroelectric system provided the only access to the Middle Fork of the Kaweah Canyon. Beside the road, the park established the Alder Creek Checking Station and ranger residence. On the far side of the canyon can be seen the Mount Whitney Power Company flume.

With the opening of the new highway in 1926, the park headquarters were relocated to a new, year-round site near the old Alder Creek Checking Station—now renamed Ash Mountain.

At Ash Mountain, the park established its headquarters and administration building, and the once-sleepy outpost became the center of park management. The site of the administration building (pictured above and below) is now a picnic area across from the present-day Foothills Visitor Center.

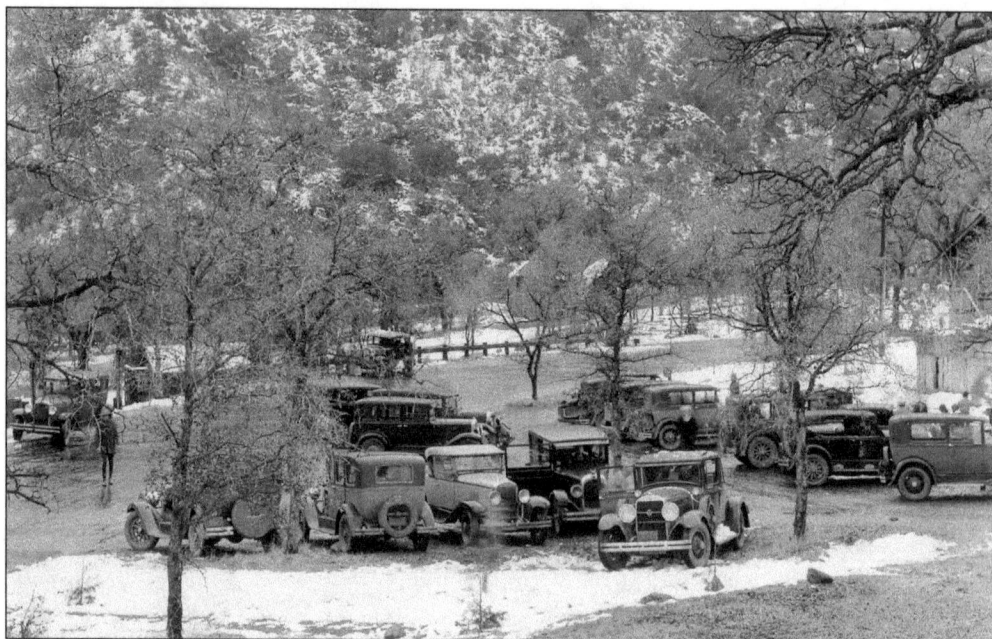

With a complex of some 20 houses for park employees and their families, pathways, landscaping, and a playground, the NPS landscape architects built a village in the blue and live oak woodland. Ash Mountain also became a popular stopping-off point on the long trip to the Giant Forest as a picnic spot (in rare snow, above) and for its radiator watering station (below). With the coming of the Great Depression in the early 1930s, park visitation decreased slightly, and funding slowed substantially, but public parks remained a relatively inexpensive escape. The superintendent reported that, in one year, the park received 15,000 applications for employment.

By the end of the 1920s, the park was basing all of its activities in this single location. A maintenance yard for the storage of park vehicles and heavy equipment was established at Ash Mountain.

The maintenance facilities, the grease rack, and the auto shop were also located at Ash Mountain.

The park also established a nursery here and greatly expanded its program of plant propagation. In the mid-1930s, the park began to replant areas in the Giant Forest, replacing bare ground with forest duff and planting young trees and shrubs.

Despite the fact that it grows to be the largest tree on earth, the sequoia germinates from a seed the approximate size of a flake of oatmeal. This four-inch-high seedling is about one year old.

WORK IN THE C.C.C.

BY HERBERT JUNER

..WINTER SPORTS - ROADS & TRAILS
..CAMP GROUNDS - FISH PLANTING
..FIRE PREVENTION - CONSERVATION

..MOUNTAIN TRANSPORTATION
..TRUCK - PACK ANIMALS

..WINTER SPORTS DEVELOPEMENT
..FISH BREEDING PONDS

10,000 FOOT HIGH TRAILS

..FIGHTING FIRES .. FOREST PROTECTION

FOOT & HORSE TRAIL ..

TELEPHONE LINE ..

..SCENIC PARK AREAS MADE ACCESSIBLE

..NEW ROADS

..FIRE WAY

..communICATION

..FIRE TRUCKS

FORESTS VIRGIN

TRAIL TO PROTECT OUR VIRGIN

PAVEMENT BUILDING CONSTRUCTION

..HAND RAILING CONSTRUCTION ON MORO ROCK FOR SAFETY & CONVENIENCE OF VISITORS
..SCENIC

..SAFER - BETTER ROADS

In 1933, Pres. Franklin Delano Roosevelt announced the formation of the Civilian Conservation Corps (CCC). In its first year, five camps with more than 1,100 enrollees were established in and around Sequoia National Park. This CCC poster does not exaggerate the variety of work undertaken by the enrollees. By 1936, the superintendent reported on the complete integration of the CCC into park administration: "Although at least four CCC companies were in the park throughout the year, no separate mention of their work need be made as they function as part of the regular park organization and practically every matter touched upon in this report has had its share of CCC participation."

There were several large, year-round CCC camps in the foothills—the first, Potwisha, was constructed on the site of a park campground and former Native American village; Buckeye, built on the site of the old hydroelectric construction camp; and Yucca Creek, seen here, at the confluence of the creek and the North Fork of the Kaweah River below the Old Colony Mill Road. Just above the bridge, in the trees beside Yucca Creek, is the old homestead of pioneer Abraham Burdick. A consumptive from New York, Burdick had wandered up the North Fork in the late 1860s, by his own account, to die in peace. After spending a year living in the open air—and making a full recovery—he purchased the 160 acres, which he farmed for the next 70 years. Upon his death, he willed his property to CCC foreman John Gruningen, who later sold it to the park.

There were also temporary tent camps throughout the park called "stump camps." Enrollees stayed at one at Emerald Lake while working on the Watchtower Trail above Lodgepole.

Some of the heaviest labor undertaken by the CCC was the construction of an extensive system of administrative fire-control roads. In the withering summer heat of the foothills, the corps constructed over 60 miles of road.

The CCC also provided valuable administrative support. One enrollee, Herbert Junep, produced the first written history of the park. Daniel Tobin (standing left, below), the park's assistant superintendent, oversees a group of enrollees in the increasingly crowded headquarters building.

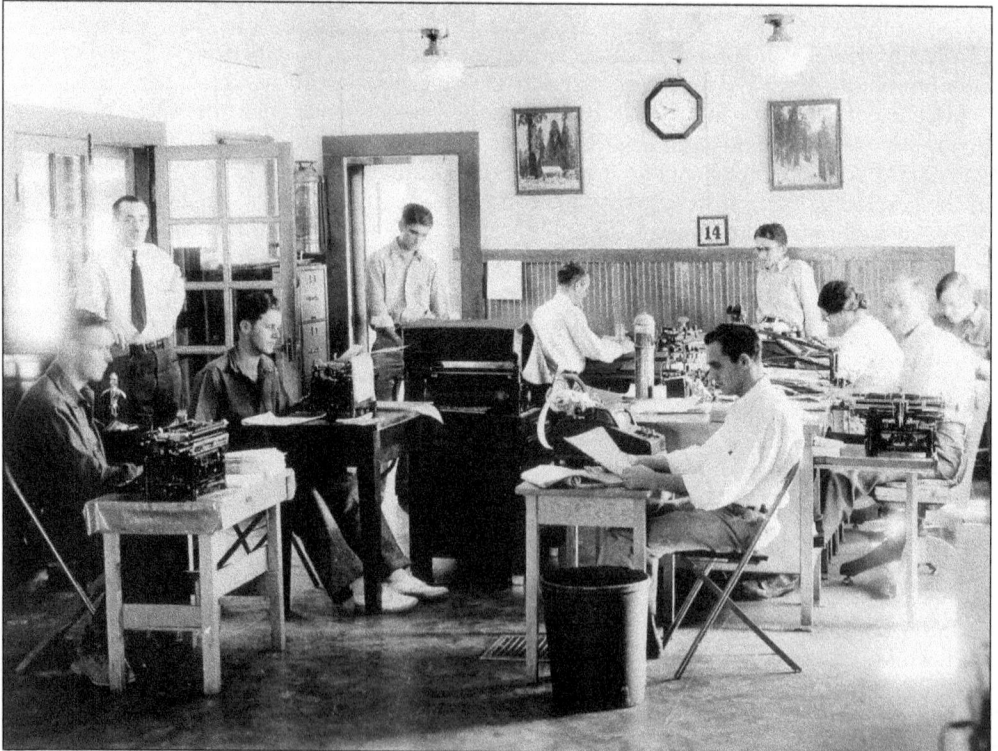

Some of the most significant conservation undertaken by the corps was the extensive landscaping that completely redefined the park's developed areas. In addition to the esthetic improvement, the work defined roadways and pathways, and contributed greatly to the increasingly conscious attempts to minimize the trampling, compacted soil, and erosion that can result from heavy visitation.

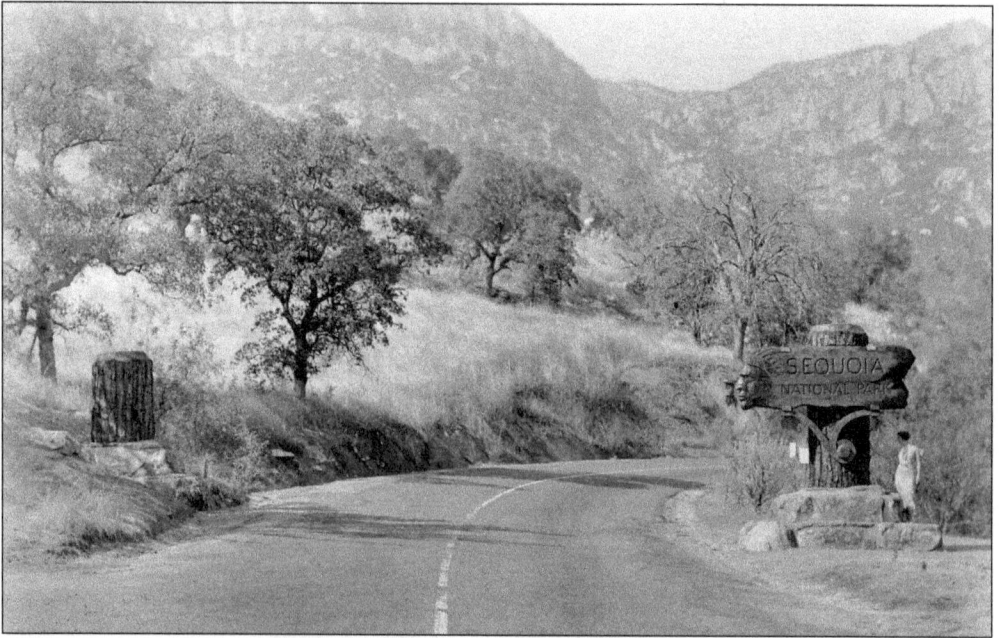

An enrollee from the nearby town of Lindsay, George Muno, carved the Indian Head entrance sign in 1935. Stationed at Potwisha Camp, Muno worked a variety of jobs, starting with kitchen patrol (KP) duty and then progressing to dining-room attendant, road worker, truck driver, and then tool and supply clerk. The enrollees were offered classes in their off time; it was in one of these that Muno's skill as a woodcarver became known. With a buffalo nickel as his model, Muno created a sign that has been admired and photographed by tens of millions of park visitors. It is listed on the National Register of Historic Places.

In its first half-century, Sequoia National Park was transformed from a region known only to a few to a well-known tourist destination. As acting superintendent Henry Clarke had suggested in 1899, the forest was now available to be "known and seen and felt by an admiring people."

On October 2, 1940, the park's 50th anniversary was celebrated at the Civic Auditorium in Visalia. Among the 600 attendees were all three of the park's civilian superintendents and one from the military era, Col. Henry Clarke. After a dinner of crab-stuffed avocado, squab *a la parisienne*, fresh peas, and potatoes pompadour, the wives of the superintendents cut a five-tiered birthday cake prepared by the baker for the Giant Forest Lodge, William Koenig (below, left). The keynote speaker was the new director of the park service, Newton Drury. He said, "Each national park in that collection of gems which now encircles the nation has its own charm, its own atmosphere or essential attribute. The Sequoia National Park is the forest primeval. Along the cool and scented lanes of the forest, man may best refresh his soul."

Drury concluded his remarks by reflecting on the challenges facing a natural park. "A delicate balance, constantly shifting, has to be struck between use and preservation. Every great landscape carries in its beauty and popularity the seeds of its own destruction. Primitive wilderness characteristics in the great national parks give them their real prestige, and will increasingly add to their distinction as these qualities disappear elsewhere under the heavy hand of man in a mechanized civilization. In large measure they have been thus far preserved. But they are under constant threat. The beauty of a virgin forest, or of a mountain lake or meadow; the setting from which great manifestations of nature's forces are viewed—these are fragile things. It is easy to rob them of their bloom, to take away much of their meaning. What was once hallowed ground becomes just another piece of real estate. And thus we lose a priceless possession of the nation."

BIBLIOGRAPHY

Browning, Peter. *Place Names of the Sierra Nevada: From Abbot to Zumwalt*. Berkeley, CA: The Wilderness Press, 1991.

Dilsaver, Lary M., and William C. Tweed. *Challenge of the Big Trees: A Resource History of Sequoia and Kings Canyon National Parks*. Three Rivers, CA: Sequoia Natural History Association, 1990.

Elliott, W. W. *A Guide to the Grand and Sublime Scenery of the Sierra Nevada in the Region about Mount Whitney*. Introduction by James B. Snyder. Emeryville, CA: Havilah Press, 2006.

Farquhar, Francis. *History of the Sierra Nevada*. Berkeley, CA: University of California Press, 1965.

Gunsky, Frederic, ed. *South of the Yosemite: Selected Writings of John Muir*. Berkeley, CA: Wilderness Press, 1968.

Hall, Ansel. *Guide to the Giant Forest, Sequoia National Park*. Yosemite, CA: self-published, 1921.

Hartesveldt, Richard J., et al. *The Giant Sequoia of the Sierra Nevada*. Washington, D.C.: National Park Service, 1975.

Hittel, John S. *The Resources of California, Comprising Agriculture, Mining, Geography, Climate, Commerce, Etc., and the Past and Future Developments of the State*. San Francisco, CA: A. Roman and Company, 1863.

Jackson, Louise A. *Mineral King: The Story of Beulah*. Three Rivers, CA: Sequoia Natural History Association, 2006.

Johnston, Verna. *Sierra Nevada: the Naturalist's Companion*. Berkeley, CA: University of California Press, 1998.

King, Clarence. *Mountaineering in the Sierra Nevada*. Yosemite, CA: Yosemite Association, 1997.

Kruska, Dennis G. *Sierra Nevada Big Trees: History of the Exhibitions, 1850–1903*. Los Angeles Dawson's Book Shop, 1985.

Muir, John. *Our National Parks*. Foreword by Alfred Runte. San Francisco, CA: Sierra Club Books, 1991.

O'Connell, Jay. *Co-Operative Dreams: A History of the Kaweah Colony*. Van Nuys, CA: Raven River Press, 1999.

Strong, Douglas H. *From Pioneers to Preservationists: A Brief History of Sequoia and Kings Canyon National Parks*. Three Rivers, CA: Sequoia Natural History Association, 2000.

Willard, Dwight. *A Guide to the Sequoia Groves of California*. Yosemite, CA: Yosemite Association, 2000.

Visit us at
arcadiapublishing.com